See how they grow
Horses and Ponies

Kathryn Walker

WAYLAND

First published in 2007
by Wayland

Copyright © Wayland 2007

Wayland
338 Euston Road
London NW1 3BH

Wayland Australia
Hachette Children's Books
Level 17/207 Kent Street
Sydney, NSW 2000

British Library Cataloguing in Publication Data
Walker, Kathryn, 1957-
    Horses & ponies. - (See how they grow)
    1. Horses - Juvenile literature 2. Ponies -
    Juvenile literature 3. Foals - Juvenile
    literature
    I. Title
    636.1'07

ISBN 13: 978 0 7502 5254 6

Printed in China

Wayland is a division of Hachette Children's Books,
an Hachette Livre UK company.

The publishers would like to thank the following
for allowing us to reproduce their pictures in
this book:
Corbis: 6, 8 (Michael Short/Robert Harding
World Imagery), 15, 17 (Kit Houghton).
Cotswold Photography: 23 (Godfrey Bragg).
Discovery Picture Library: 9. FLPA: cover,
title page, 14 and 21 (PGM Pictures), 5 (David
Hosking). Getty images: 4 (Jerry Young/Dorling
Kindersley collection), 7 (Bernard Fuchs), 10
(Sisse Brimberg/National Geographic), 18 and 20
(David Handley/Dorling Kindersley). Istockphoto:
11, 12 (Jeff Clow), 16 (Barry Crossley).
Kath Walker: 19.

Contents

Horse or pony?

Horses and ponies are the same type of animal. A pony is a small horse. It measures 1.5 metres or less when fully grown. Anything taller is called a horse.

▼ Height is the main difference between a horse and a pony. This pony is one of the smallest types. It is called a Shetland.

horse

pony

Ponies and horses are measured from the ground to the top of the **withers**. Withers are the high part of the horse's back.

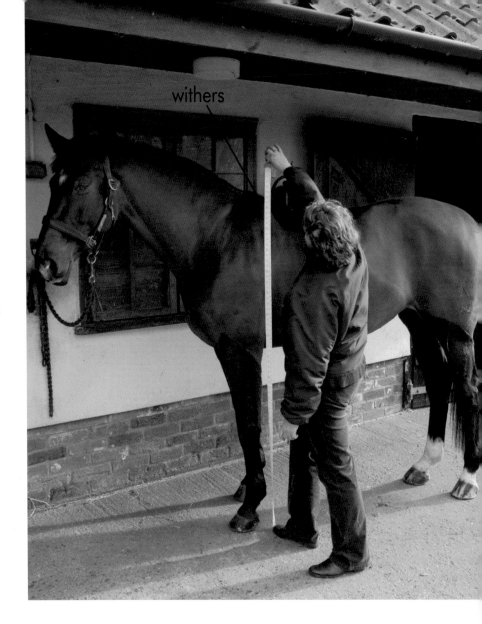

withers

Horse Fact

Horses and ponies are measured in '**hands**'. A hand is a measure of 10 centimetres.

▲ A horse measures more than 14 hands and 2 inches (1.5 metres) from the ground to the withers.

Wild and domestic

Wild horses and ponies live in groups called **herds**. They spend their days looking for food and **grazing**. Most horses and ponies are **domestic**. This means that they are kept by people.

▼ These are wild mustang horses. They are found in the western United States.

People have kept horses and ponies for thousands of years. In the past, people used them to pull heavy loads. Horses and ponies were also the main form of **transport**. These days, people keep them mainly for pleasure or sport.

▲ People used to travel in carriages like this, pulled by horses.

Different shapes and sizes

Horses and ponies come in all shapes and sizes. There are special types called **breeds**. The fastest breed of horse is the thoroughbred. It is best known as a racehorse. The tallest breed is the Shire. This strong horse can pull heavy loads.

▼ For many centuries, the Shire horse was used for farm work.

8

Ponies make good riding horses for children. Welsh ponies and Connemaras are two popular breeds. Many ponies are a mixture of different breeds.

▲ Ponies are smaller than horses. This makes them easier for children to handle and ride.

A foal is born

A female horse has just one baby at a time. For the first year of its life, the baby horse or pony is called a **foal**. A foal can stand up when it is just an hour or two old.

▼ When a foal is born, the mother licks it clean.

The foal feeds on its mother's milk until it is about six months old. The foal also starts to nibble hay and grains when it is a couple of weeks old.

▲ For the first weeks of its life, a foal gets the food it needs from its mother's milk.

Growing up

A male horse or pony under four years old is called a **colt**. A female is called a **filly**. A horse or pony is grown-up when it is about four.

Horses and ponies normally live for between 20 and 30 years. Some live for more than 40 years.

Horse Fact

A grown-up female horse is called a **mare**. The male is either called a **stallion** or a **gelding**.

▲ Horses and ponies are usually trained to carry riders when they are about three years old.

▼ Foals like to play and run together. Play is a way of exercising and learning.

Understanding horses and ponies

A horse or pony likes to be with other horses or ponies. It will form special friendships with some horses. There may also be others that they dislike.

◀ Horses that are friends will greet each other by touching and **grooming** (cleaning).

▲ These horses are fighting with each other. Standing up on the back legs like this is called rearing.

Caring for horses and ponies

Many horses and ponies live outdoors all year. Some spend their nights in stables. Others also spend part of their days indoors. These horses need to have exercise every day.

Rolling is good exercise for horses. It is also a way of scratching an itch.

Horses and ponies in fields have grass to eat. In the cold weather there is not enough grass for them so they need hay to eat. Horses in stables have all their food and water brought to them.

▲ Stables need to be cleaned every day. This is called mucking out.

Learning to ride

The safest way of learning to ride is to take riding lessons. You will learn how to control a pony and learn about **tack**. Tack is equipment you put on the horse before riding it.

It is important to wear the right clothes for riding. These will keep you comfortable and safe. A rider must wear a hard hat to protect the head.

▲ These children are at riding school. Exercises like this will help them to sit safely on horseback.

riding hat

saddle

bridle

reins

> The main pieces of tack are the saddle and bridle. They help you to control the horse.

riding boots

19

Owning a horse or pony

Horses and ponies need exercise and grooming every day. Keeping a pony is fun, but takes up a lot of time. It can also cost a lot of money.

▼ Grooming helps keep your horse or pony healthy.

Horses and ponies need metal horseshoes to protect their feet. A **farrier** will fit these shoes. The shoes need replacing every few weeks.

Horse Fact

The hooves of a horse or pony grow all the time, like people's fingernails.

▶ A farrier has to trim and file a horse's hoof before fitting a horseshoe.

Fun with horses and ponies

Riding a horse or pony can be great fun. You might also enjoy showjumping or competing in **gymkhanas**. A gymkhana is an event with games and races on horseback.

▼ Riding through the countryside like this is called hacking.

In showjumping, horses have to jump over a series of fences. Skill and speed is important in these competitions.

Glossary

breed
A special kind of horse or pony. Horses or ponies in this group are very alike. This is because their parents belonged to the same group.

colt
Male horse that is less than four years old.

domestic horse
Horse or pony that is kept by people.

farrier
A person who makes and fits horseshoes.

filly
Female horse that is less than four years old.

foal
A horse or pony that is less than one year old.

gelding
A male horse that has been gelded. Gelding is an operation that stops the horse being able to father foals.

grazing
Eating grass in a field.

grooming
Brushing and cleaning a horse or pony.

gymkhana
Competition with games and races on horseback.

hand
A unit used for measuring horses and ponies. A hand is 10 centimetres. This is about the width of a man's hand.

herd
A group of horses.

mare
A grown-up female horse or pony.

stable
Building where a horse can be sheltered and fed.

stallion
A grown-up male horse or pony. Unlike a gelding, a stallion can father foals.

tack
Equipment put on to a horse or pony. This equipment makes it easier to handle or ride the horse.

transport
Moving about from one place to another.

withers
The highest part of a horse's back at the base of its neck.

Index